Dela Kienle

Plastic

And how to live without it.

Illustrations by Horst Hellmeier

Ragged Bears

Plastic – a bane and a blessing

We live in a world of plastic. Your trainers, biros, and toothbrushes are entirely or partly made of plastic, as are your fleeces and raincoats. Plastic is found in the majority of supermarket packaging, in smartphones and computers, under the bonnet of cars: it's virtually everywhere!

Plastic is a great, versatile material. But we use it without thinking. And now huge quantities of rubbish pollute the oceans. Increasingly, scientists are also finding tiny microplastics in drinking water, on fields and in the air we breathe. This is not surprising: after all, we are producing huge quantities of plastic, around 22 times more than 50 years ago.

AMOUNT OF
PLASTIC IN 1964 ...

And if mankind continues along this path, we will have produced an enormous plastic mountain by the year 2050: a total of 34 billion tons of plastic.

... BY 2050

The basic problem is we use most of the plastic only once and then throw it away immediately. A plastic bag, for example, is only used for an average of 25 minutes. And nearly half of the plastic we produce is used for packaging and ends up in the bin after use. But because plastic is so durable, it is very hard to get rid of it. We can recycle or burn some of the plastic waste. But it looks like the rest will remain on Earth for hundreds of years.

What are we using plastic for in Europe?

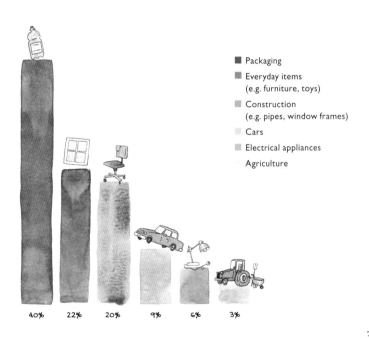

- Packaging
- Everyday items (e.g. furniture, toys)
- Construction (e.g. pipes, window frames)
- Cars
- Electrical appliances
- Agriculture

40%   22%   20%   9%   6%   3%

Wanted: a miracle substance!

Let's travel back in time, to around 120 years ago. There was no
plastic then. Items for everyday use were made from wood or metal;
buttons were made from animal horn, and combs
from tortoise shells. In those days even a
toothbrush was a luxury item only rich
people could afford. Therefore, more
and more chemists were trying
to find a cheaper substitute for
natural materials.

They were looking for a kind of miracle substance: it needed to be
pliable, light, stable and easy to manufacture. They mixed hundreds
of substances in their labs, experimented with pressure and different
temperatures. All in vain! Then, finally, the Belgian-American chemist
Leo Baekeland achieved a breakthrough. In 1907 he filed a patent for
Bakelite: a gooey black or brown paste that could be pressed into
nearly any shape. It was the first type of plastic that could be made
on an industrial scale – and it was a huge success!

Soon, ashtrays, telephones, and radios were made from Bakelite. But Baekeland's competitors were also on the ball: in the decades that followed, they developed countless other plastics. Some could be dyed in a particular colour, while others were pliable or transparent like glass. So there were a lot of new additions to the world of chemicals. From the 1950s onwards plastic had become a part of everyday life. Since then, many items have become mass products. For example, ladies' tights are no longer made from expensive silk, but from nylon. Even toothbrushes are no longer a luxury item. And newly developed "smart" plastics will continue to change our lives – by enabling planes to become ever lighter, houses to stay cool without air conditioning, or even synthetic shirts to repel dirt.

Become a plastic detective!

There are many different types of plastic. The difference is in their chemical composition. Some contain "agents" like softeners or hardeners. Take a look around your home. How many types of plastic can you find?

Because there are so many different types, it is difficult to recycle plastic. To make it easier to sort plastics, they are marked with these triangular recycling codes.

Name: PET (polyethylenterephthalate)
Recycling code: 01
Characteristics: PET is stable and resistant to acids.
Typical products: Drinks bottles, films, fibres for fleece jackets.

Name: PE (polyethylene)
Recycling code: 02 (high density) and 04 (low density)
Characteristics: PE is the most widely used plastic. Low density PE is pliable, high density PE is hard and robust.
Typical products: Many packaging films, bags, coatings inside drinks cartons, etc.

Name: PVC (polyvinyl chloride)
Recycling code: 03
Characteristics: There are two basic types of PVC – hard and soft. Depending on how it is made, it can be either very solid or very flexible.
Typical products: Pipes, window frames, flooring, wellies.

Name: Polypropylene
Recycling code: 05
Characteristics: It is very stable and only changes its shape when it is exposed to very high temperatures.
Typical products: Bumpers, bottle tops, margarine tubs, sportswear

Name: PS (polystyrol)
Recycling code: 06
Characteristics: In its pure form, polystyrol is transparent. But it can also be non-transparent – or expanded like polystyrene.
Typical products: Yoghurt pots, single-use dishes, jewel cases for CDs, foam trays for meat.

Name: Silicone
Recycling code: 07
Characteristics: It is heat-resistant, water repellent and flexible. With small changes to its structure, it can be made into silicone oils which are often added to shampoo and other products.
Typical products: Baking trays, dummies, sealants for bathrooms and kitchens.

07 is also used to identify all "other" types of plastics which do not have their own number – including bio plastics.

What is plastic made of?

Whether it is a Lego brick, a toilet seat or a bag, the raw material for most plastic items is crude oil. The first step is to break it down into its constituent parts. During this process, tiny building blocks called monomers are created. Then heat, pressure or chemical solutions are used to link these building blocks again into long chains called polymers. These do not occur in nature, they are man-made and also called "synthetic" materials. The polymer chains can be arranged in different ways, resulting in three different groups of plastics.

In Duroplasts, the chains are linked to form a network. These plastics are hard and do not melt. They are used for things like frying pan handles.

In Thermoplasts, the chains are only loosely wrapped around each other. When heat is applied they become detached from each other. These types of plastics can melt and harden again. They are used to manufacture bags, PET bottles or plastic films.

Elastomers are flexible and stretchy. They are used for things like rubber bands, tyres or sealing rings. Their chains form dense balls, similar to balls of wool, and disentangle when you pull on the rubber band. When you let go, the polymer chains retract into a ball.

What actually is crude oil?

It is black and greasy – but it is a precious resource. Crude oil was created in the primeval oceans: over millions of years, dead microorganisms and plants were sinking to the bottom of these oceans. Then, air-tight layers of sand and stones were deposited on top of them. The microorganisms and plants rotted and eventually transformed into crude oil. This means that it is impossible to produce new crude oil. We should, therefore, use crude oil sparingly because the reserves are running out. And when crude oil burns, it also generates carbon dioxide (CO_2). This gas is not a bad thing as such: it is also contained in the air we breathe out. Together with other "greenhouse gases", CO_2 envelopes the globe like a blanket. It keeps the heat on Earth, so it does not get lost in space, which is very cold. But now there are too many greenhouse gases because we humans are burning so much oil, coal, and natural gas. The Earth is heating up. We are already experiencing the consequences of climate change.

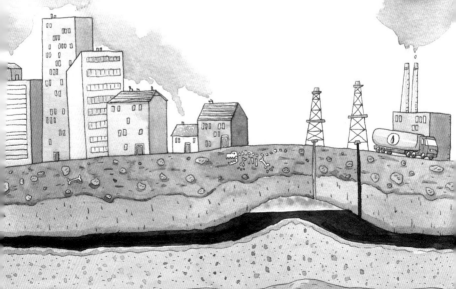

Bioplastics – good or bad?

It sounds tempting: you can read on more and more bags and packaging that they are made of bioplastics. Can you use them without feeling guilty? And what are bioplastics? This term is very confusing. If a bag is "bio", this can mean two very different things.

Option 1:

The bag is bio-based. This means that renewable resources like maize or sugar cane were used for its manufacture. However, the chemical structure is often the same as normal plastics made from oil.
In practice, the two types of materials are often mixed, such as in Bio-PET.

Option 2:

The bag is biodegradable; i.e. it will decompose after a certain period of time. It can be made from renewable resources but may also be made from oil.

Unfortunately, both options have disadvantages. To grow the raw materials you need for bioplastics, like maize, you need fertiliser, pesticides and fuel for tractors. And wouldn't it be better to use fields for growing food? Even "compostable" plastic does not rot as easily as apple peel. For example, if it lands in the cold sea it will degrade just as badly as a normal plastic bag. Bioplastics *will* degrade in an industrial composting facility… but this takes three months and a temperature of 65 degrees Celsius.

The operators of these facilities can't afford to wait that long: other types of bio waste rot much faster and each additional day costs money. Another problem is that you cannot tell whether it is normal plastic or bioplastic among the vegetable peels. So, to be on the safe side, as much plastic as possible is separated out and burnt in these facilities.

For all these reasons, the Environment Agency has come to a clear conclusion: as it stands, bioplastics are no better than ordinary plastics. Perhaps scientists will be able to solve these problems in the future. But for now, if you want to help nature, you should use less plastic... whether it is bio or not.

How long does it take for plastic to degrade?

Old leaves are a feast for microorganisms: bacteria, fungi, and worms allow the leaves to rot and transform them into precious new soil. However, there is not much these tiny organisms can do against plastics. Plastics are extremely stable. And that is a huge problem when they end up in nature. Some of them can remain in the oceans for centuries. And even if you can no longer see a plastic bag in the end, it has not degraded but broken down into tiny pieces.

What degrades quickly in the sea?

Join the waste with the correct number.

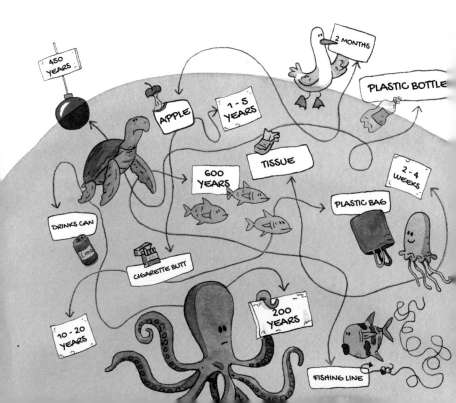

Caution: Unhealthy!

Plastics often contain additives to make them perform better in sunlight, to make them flame resistant, or feel smooth. But after a while, some of these chemicals start to escape and may even be harmful to our health. One example of a controversial substance is Bisphenol A (BPA). It is often used to coat cans to prevent them from getting rusty. And it is contained in drinks bottles or parts of dishes made from polycarbonate plastic. It is often labelled as "PC" or recycling code 7. Substances called phthalates, acting as softeners, are also problematic. They are used in soft PVC plastic which is used to make shower curtains, lilos, squeaky rubber ducks and other soft toys. Very cheap products from unknown companies often have very high levels. If you want to avoid unhealthy additives, look out for "PVC-free", "phthalate-free" and "BPA-free". The materials polyethylene (recycling codes 2 and 4) and polypropylene (recycling code 5) are considered to be unproblematic.

A sea of plastic

Approximately two thirds of the Earth are covered by water. But our wonderful oceans are turning into gigantic rubbish tips. It is estimated that there are 150 billion kilogrammes of plastic waste floating in the oceans. Every year, at least 8 billion kilogrammes of plastic are added. This is equivalent to one bin lorry full of shopping bags, drinks bottles, and packaging landing in the sea every minute. And if our use of plastic continues to increase as before it will be two bin lorries per minute by the year 2030... and as much as five bin lorries by the year 2050. Then, the plastic in the oceans will weigh more than the combined weight of all the fish!

TODAY

2050

It is estimated that about 70 percent of the plastic waste is sinking to the bottom of the sea. Other items are drifting higher up on the surface of the water. Carried by wind and currents, the plastic then reaches the ice sheets at the North Pole or the remote beaches of the South Seas. However, a large amount of plastic ends up in five gigantic "waste vortexes". They form where oceanic currents meet. The biggest is called the "Great Pacific Garbage Patch". Experts believe that it is as big as the whole of Central Europe. However, you shouldn't picture a waste vortex as a drifting waste island. The water is more like a plastic soup – only it isn't noodles floating around the soup, but a huge amount of plastic instead.

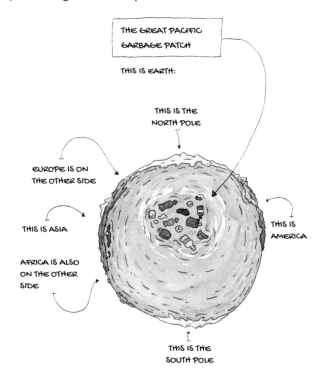

THE GREAT PACIFIC GARBAGE PATCH

THIS IS EARTH:

THIS IS THE NORTH POLE

EUROPE IS ON THE OTHER SIDE

THIS IS ASIA

AFRICA IS ALSO ON THE OTHER SIDE

THIS IS AMERICA

THIS IS THE SOUTH POLE

Microplastics: The invisible danger

When plastic lands in the sea, it breaks up into ever smaller fragments due to the impact of waves, sunlight, and friction. These "microplastics" are barely visible to the naked eye, and yet they cause huge problems! Scientists estimate that there are already up to 51 trillion micro particles drifting in the world's oceans. Many of these contain harmful substances. Microorganisms and fish, like anchovies, eat the plastic with their food and then end up in the stomachs of larger animals themselves. This continues until the plastic potentially ends up on our plates when we eat fish or mussels. Experts are currently investigating if this is harmful to our health.

Of course, you (hopefully) never dump any rubbish in nature. And yet, you are contributing to the creation of microplastics. On average, four kilogrammes of plastic particles end up in the environment for every person in the UK. Fleeces and many other items of clothing are entirely or partially made from plastic. When they go through the washing machine, they release countless fine fibres which end up in the wastewater. Some types of shampoo, face peelings, and detergents also contain tiny plastic particles. Water treatment plants cannot filter them out completely when they clean the water. And a particularly large amount of microplastics also comes off car tyres.

EXHAUST FUMES

MICROPLASTICS

Plastic dust is also released from road markings, as well as from playing fields and playgrounds with synthetic coverings or from buildings which are painted with synthetic paint. Many different things put together produce enormous amounts of microplastics. Some of these are blown away by the wind, and some of these are washed away by the rain. The plastic particles then get into rivers, through the sewers, and eventually into the sea. But scientists are now increasingly discovering them in the soil, in the drinking water, and even in the air.

Why do animals eat plastic?

As sea birds, fulmars circle far out above the North Sea to catch fish. But now, they often accidentally swallow plastic. This gave scientists an idea: the more waste is found in the birds' stomachs, the more polluted the oceans are. This is why they examine as many of the fulmars that wash up dead on the North Sea coast as possible.

The result is really alarming: approximately 98 percent of the birds have plastic in their stomachs. But many other sea animals also suffer from the increased pollution of the oceans. Studies have shown that plastic waste gives off a smell, which is perceived as the scent of food by some birds. Turtles, on the other hand, mistake floating plastic bags for tasty jellyfish. This mainly affects young turtles because they tend to stay closer to the coast and the water's surface, where a lot of waste is drifting.

Once the stomach of an animal is filled with the remains of balloons or bags, threads from fishing nets or other waste, there is not much room left for proper food. The animals starve with a full stomach. Or they are so weakened that they become sick more easily. Plastic waste also damages coral reefs and other habitats at the bottom of the sea. Drifting microplastics are also harmful. Experiments have shown that oysters have markedly fewer offspring than normal if they regularly filter plastic crumbs from the water. Another serious problem is that curious seals, dolphins, and other animals are getting caught in drifting plastic; for example, in lost fishing nets. Many of them drown immediately. Others must continue to swim with plastic rings over their snouts, or with constricted fins.

But how does the plastic get into the sea?

Through rivers

Especially in poorer countries, plastic waste is often not burned or recycled, but ends up in open rubbish dumps or directly on the street. From there, the wind can easily blow it into rivers, from where the plastic is then washed into the sea. Eight of the ten most polluted rivers are in Asia. But a crisp bag that someone carelessly throws away in the UK can also end up in the sea – via the rivers.

From cities

Tiny microplastic particles unintentionally get into the wastewater and, from there, into rivers and oceans. Some of these are fibres from synthetic clothing which are released during washing. Some of the microplastics have come off car tyres and the soles of shoes. Or they are contained in shampoos, toothpaste, and other toiletries.

From beaches

Billions of people go to the seaside for a holiday; unfortunately, many of them do not care about the environment and simply leave their rubbish behind. Bottles, bags, sweet wrappers, straws, single-use cutlery, food trays... enormous amounts of plastic from beaches end up directly in the water.

From ships

Of course, this is banned. But many ships still dump their waste into the water. And sometimes, it happens that cargo ships lose part of their load. During a storm in January 2019, for example, 270 containers slid into the North Sea.

Through fishermen

It is estimated that up to a quarter of the plastic waste in the oceans consists of huge "ghost nets". These are nets that tore loose from fishing boats. Sometimes, illegal fishermen also cut their nets on purpose to escape inspection. The plastic nets are very robust and continue to catch fish indefinitely – turning them into deadly traps for animals!

Can the oceans be cleaned?

It sounds virtually impossible. But more and more people are determined to fish as much plastic out of the oceans as possible. And they are really inventive!

The ocean cleaner

Boyan Slat designed his first sea cleaning system as a school project. The young man from the Netherlands is now head of the organisation "The Ocean Cleanup". His idea: why should we chase after the plastic, if it can come to us? "The Ocean Cleanup" wants to set approx. 1000 m long pipes adrift in the largest garbage patch. These "tentacles" are shaped like a horseshoe. As the plastic waste moves faster than the Cleanup system, it drifts up to the barrier, accumulates there and can then be captured by a ship. The first "tentacle" has already been set adrift, but, unfortunately, it didn't work. The engineers are now working on a better version. The plan is to eventually have dozens of waste catchers drifting in the oceans.

The ghost net divers

In Europe alone, around 25,000 fishing nets with a total length of 1250 kilometres are lost each year. They will continue to drift in the water and kill animals for centuries unless someone removes them from the water. The "Ghost Fishing" foundation encourages volunteer divers worldwide to remove these nets, even though it is often difficult and dangerous. If possible, the nets will be recycled back on land.

They are turned into tear-resistant yarn which is then used for manufacturing socks, swimming costumes, and carpets.

The waste fishermen

Fishermen do not just catch cod and haddock in their nets, but also loads of plastic. Normally, they throw the waste back overboard. The "Fishing for litter" campaign distributes large, robust sacks among fishermen, and ensures that they can easily hand over the waste, free of charge, on their return to port. In the UK alone, 380 vessels are now taking part in the campaign.

THAT WAS A GOOD CATCH TODAY

PLASTIC WASTE

How to deal with old plastic?

Compared to other European countries, the UK produces a lot of plastic waste and the quantity has been increasing every year! At least, we collect most of it through our waste system, and **99** percent of the plastic is "salvaged". However, this sounds better than it actually is: because more than half of the plastic ends up in an incinerator. Burning waste does generate heat or electricity, but it also means that the gas CO_2 is emitted, which is harmful to the climate. Also the precious resource crude oil is lost, which cannot be recovered. It is much better to recycle plastic. However, with current technology, this is not easy as there are many different types. And often, the plastics are joined with or stuck to other materials. In meat packaging, for example, the tray is often made from polypropylene, whereas the film that covers it is made from wafer-thin layers of PET and polyethylene. Even if you throw this type of packaging into the recycling bin, it is difficult to separate the individual types of plastic in the waste facility. Even if "mixed plastics" can be recycled, the result will be an inferior material which can be made into things like park benches – but not a new food container.

IN MY FORMER LIFE I WAS A MEAT TRAY

WOOF

EU politicians are demanding that, by 2030, all packaging should be produced in a way that makes all plastics easy to reuse. That would be great. Of course, recycling is very important, but it would be even better if we could avoid all this waste in the first place.

Join in the plastic challenge!

We can all try to use less plastic in our everyday lives. How about turning this into a challenge – a competition with your friends, family or classmates? It's really easy. Think about how long you want to do your "plastic fasting" for. Then decide on five (or seven! or ten!) pledges that enable you to save plastic. Write them down on a piece of paper, put it up where you can see it... and get started! Write down every day which pledge worked well and which pledge you found difficult. Your friends can do their challenges at the same time. Or you "nominate" them when you have finished yours and you can talk about your experiences. Good luck!

Of course, you won't be able to give up plastic altogether. You don't need to. But it will help you discover how much (unnecessary) plastic you use in your everyday life and you can inspire others with your campaign.

Parents often have good reasons why they buy individual products or why they go to particular shops. But they will definitely support you when they see how much effort you put into your "plastic fasting"!

Don't let it put you off if some children laugh at you. It is great that you are doing something to help nature. You are helping to make the world a better place! And those who just turn up their noses don't understand how serious the situation has become.

My plastic challenge

Name:

This is how long I want to do my "plastic fasting" for:

This is what I am doing already:

My pledges for the challenge:

This is what I want to carry on doing
after the challenge:

30 tips for using less plastic

Shopping

1.) Say no to plastic bags!

We are getting better, but in the
UK, people are still asking for
1.1 billion shopping bags at the checkout every
year. This is an average of 20 bags per person per year.
Why not take a bag or a rucksack with you when you go
shopping? You can use these again and again and again.

What is better for nature?

First impressions can be misleading: some things sound as
if they would be environmentally friendly, but once experts
calculate all the advantages and disadvantages, it doesn't always
look so good. Carrier bags made from paper, which are offered
instead of plastic bags in many shops, are an example of this.
As they need to be very strong, it takes a lot of energy
and water to manufacture them. Paper bags are only more
ecological than plastic bags if they are used at least four times.
Even a cloth bag only has a better "environmental footprint"
if it is used at least 25 times.

2.) Choose unpackaged fruit and vegetables!

Cucumbers in a plastic wrap, tomatoes in a plastic tray:
more and more fruit and vegetables are packaged.
But there is often a choice, even in normal
supermarkets. But a lot more unpackaged
fruit and vegetables are available in
wholefood shops and at weekly markets.

MAKE YOUR OWN: Recycling bag

Take an old T-shirt and turn it inside out. Cut off (as shown in drawing 1)
the sleeves, the collar, and the seam at the bottom. You will need
tassels at the bottom: make straight cuts, approx. 10cm long, for your
tassels. Then tie two opposite tassels with
a firm double knot until they are
all done (drawing 2). To finish,
turn the bag inside out so
that all the knots are on
the inside.

CUT ALL OF THESE OFF   MAKE 10 CM CUTS   TIE INTO KNOTS

3.) Avoid "vest carrier bags"!

The thin plastic bags for vegetables often have handles like a vest.
Hence their funny name. They are free, but generate a lot of rubbish.
You can place peppers, tomatoes or apples on the conveyor belt at
the checkout without a bag or place them in a reusable net.

4.) No complex packaging!

Take a look at your fridge and your storage shelves with your parents: which types of plastic packaging are particularly complex? For example: are they made of thick plastic or foam? Multiple layers of packaging? Lots of packaging and only a very small amount inside?

When you go shopping, see if you can find products with simpler packaging, they will still taste good! Perhaps your favourite cheese is not only available shrink-wrapped, but also fresh on the counter, where the shop assistant only wraps it in coated paper?

5.) Make your own sweets!

Gummi bears, crisps, chocolate bars and biscuits; sweet treats often come packaged in plastic. Think about whether you (sometimes) want to go without them. You can bake your own biscuits or cakes, or even make your own fruit gum – it's easy.

MAKE YOUR OWN: Wine gums

Pour 100 millilitres of fruit juice into a small saucepan.
Add 6 teaspoons of powdered gelatine or 8 gelatine leaves
(or a vegetarian/vegan substitute) and let it soak for five minutes.
Add 1 or 2 tablespoons of sugar and 1 tablespoon of lemon juice.
Then heat the mixture until the gelatine has dissolved. Do not let
it boil! Pour the mixture into a deep plate and let it set for two
hours. Then you can cut it into small cubes. Your wine gums do
not contain any preservatives, so you need to eat them within a
few days.

6.) Avoid mini portions!

There is a trend towards ever smaller
packs or portions. They are popular
with single adults – and children.
They are the target audience for many
of the products: mini fruit yoghurts in
colourful pots, probiotic yoghurt in
small drinking bottles, fruit puree in
plastic squeeze pouches, individually
wrapped biscuits… They are all handy
if you are on the go, but they create a
lot of rubbish.

7.) Sneezing without plastic!

Ten tissues inside a plastic pack. And these are then sealed in a larger pack. But tissues in box dispensers are also available. They are great to use at home and when you are on the go! In the old days people used handkerchiefs and washed them after use. Perhaps, this is also a good idea for today?

8.) Buy fresh from the bakery!

Rolls from the supermarket that you can reheat at home are handy, but they come in a thick plastic wrapper. You could go to the bakery instead. And you can take a clean cloth bag with you and put the rolls in there.

9.) Choose your yoghurt carefully!

Go for yoghurt that comes in a glass rather than a plastic pot. You can make your own yoghurt without any packaging.

MAKE YOUR OWN: Natural yoghurt

Get an adult to give you a hand. Fill a thermos flask with very hot water to "preheat" it and keep it closed for an hour. Then heat 500 millilitres of milk in a saucepan to a temperature of about 40°C. Stir in 50 g of bought natural yoghurt. Empty the water from the thermos flask and add the milk mixture. Wrap a towel around the flask and place it in a warm corner for 12 to 24 hours without lifting or shaking it. The milk will have turned to yoghurt. You can keep it in the fridge for five days and sweeten it with jam or honey, if you prefer.

10.) Do not spit chewing gum onto the street!

Most chewing gums are actually a mixture of synthetic substances. This is why they will stay on the road for many years. In some cities there are up to 90 wads of chewing gum per square metre stuck to the ground. It takes a lot of energy to remove them. But, if a chewing gum has just been spat out, it might be eaten by animals and they could die from constipation. Therefore, always wrap your chewing gum in paper and throw it in the bin!

WHAT'S THAT?

IT LOOKS YUMMY.

Bathroom & clothing

11.) Clean soap!

Shower gel always comes in plastic
bottles. Many families also use liquid
soap to wash their hands and throw away the
dispenser as soon as it is empty. A better
solution is to refill the soap dispenser
(there are increasing numbers of shops
where this is possible e.g. your local
health shop) or simply replace it
with a normal, nice-smelling bar of
soap without any plastic.

12.) Toiletries without any microplastics

Some toiletries still contain plastics. This is either in the form of tiny
visible beads, or they can be invisible, hiding in binding or filling agents.

This applies to some types of toothpaste, shower
gel, sun cream, face peelings, and shampoo.
It helps to take a closer look at the ingredients,
which are usually printed very small! The following
complicated words mean: Caution, microplastics!
Polyethylene (PE), polypropylene (PP), polystyrene
(PS), polyethylene terephthalate (PET), nylon-12,
nylon-6, polyurethane (PUR), acrylates copolymer
(AC), acrylate crosspolymer (ACS), polyacrylate
(PA), polymethyl methacrylate (PMMA).

13.) Take a closer look at your clothes!

Many items of clothing and shoes are made entirely or partially from plastic. Of course, a warm fleece jacket or sportswear that dries quickly is useful. But every time these are washed, plastic fibres end

up in the water cycle. Perhaps you could choose biological natural fibres instead, like cotton and wool? The most important thing is to only buy clothes if you need them and will wear them regularly. And if they don't fit you anymore, you should pass them onto younger children. Often, you can find really exciting clothes at car boot sales and in second-hand shops.

14.) Choose quality!

Sometimes, you need something new; for example, an alarm clock or a rucksack. There is often a choice, and you can see if something is made from (a lot of) plastic or a different material. Above all, make sure that the item you buy will last; no cheap rubbish that breaks straight away and gets thrown away. Buying things second hand is particularly good for the environment. You should use the plastic products you already own as long as possible and repair them.

School

15.) Protect your exercise books and textbooks without using plastic!

You can use thick recycled paper, brown paper or a double layer of newspaper to protect your textbooks. Talk to your teacher: why do exercise books need to be covered in sticky-back plastic or be laminated? Teachers often think this is necessary to protect the exercise books. Perhaps your class can find a different way to protect them; for example, wrap them in recycled or brown paper and then colour code them so you can tell them apart more easily.

16.) Make your schoolbag environmentally friendly!

It's no use sorting out everything made from plastic and throwing it away. Continue to use what you already have. But you could consider the environment when you need to buy new things for school: you can get pencil sharpeners made from metal, wooden rulers, ball point pens made from cardboard ... glue is available in refillable bottles... there are pencil cases made from leather or cotton... erasers made from natural rubber... and wooden pencils colour just as well as felt tip pens, which always dry out quickly anyway.

DRAT, MY FELT-TIP PEN DRIED UP AGAIN.

MY PENCIL STILL WORKS.

17.) Enjoy lunchtimes without plastic!

Put your lunch in a reusable container, ideally made from metal. That's better than cling film, aluminium foil or disposable bags made from paper or plastic. Are you taking any other snacks to school? Are they sealed in plastic? You could take a Muesli bar, they are easy to make at home and add to your lunch box.

MAKE YOUR OWN: Muesli bars

Chop 75 g of dried fruit and nuts as finely as possible. Mix them with 180 g of porridge oats, 2 tablespoons of ground almonds, 1 pinch of salt, and 1 teaspoon of sesame seeds. In a saucepan, heat 7 tablespoons of vegetable oil with 5 tablespoons of maple syrup, agave nectar or similar. Do not let the mixture get too hot! Mix in the dry ingredients. Place a sheet of baking paper in a shallow tin and add the Muesli mixture. Press it down well and place it in the fridge for 30 minutes. Then, the mixture will have set and you can lift it out of the tin and cut it into small Muesli bars.

Drinking

18.) Drink tap water!

Tap water is the most environmentally-friendly drink. It is strictly controlled, its composition is as good as mineral water bought in a shop, and it does not need to be bottled and transported. And the price of tap water is unbeatable! If you like sparkling water you can make your own with a SodaStream. And if people choose to buy mineral water they should go for returnable bottles where possible, and ideally water that has been bottled as near as possible to where you live. Glass bottles can be re-used up to 50 times, returnable plastic bottles up to 20 times. There are already deposit return systems for bottles in other countries, and there are now plans to introduce a similar system in the UK.

All over the world, people are buying more than 1 million plastic bottles every minute. This generates a huge amount of rubbish. Germany is one of the few countries that charges a deposit on single-use bottles. This is why most people there take them back to the shop. PET is easy to recycle. However, the process uses a lot of energy. The shredded plastic is often used to make textile fibres for clothing. On average, a fleece contains 16 used PET drinks bottles.

19.) Bring a bottle!

Do you get thirsty in school, or during exercise? Then take a reusable drinks bottle with you. They are available in metal or glass, with a protective cloth cover. Avoid drinks cartons. Some of them are entirely made of plastic; some of them are made of plastic-coated cardboard and they come with a straw. In any case, they generate a lot of rubbish.

20.) "No straw for me, please!"

This is how friends of the environment order a drink. In the UK alone, we use approx. 40 billion plastic straws per year. They are among the items most frequently found on beaches. In the EU,

NO STRAW FOR ME, PLEASE!

they will be banned from 2021. Alternatives made from cardboard or bamboo have been available for a while. But these also use energy and raw materials for their manufacture and generate more rubbish, so it's best to avoid straws.

Toys

21.) Be more aware when choosing toys!

Hardly anybody is against using Lego or Playmobil; toys that are used by children over many years and can be passed on to younger children. But, perhaps there are a lot of plastic odds and ends accumulating in your room: cheap items that get broken after a short while, and that you don't get much use out of. You get them after birthday parties, at the funfair – or you buy them yourself because it looks fun on a magazine or maybe it's in fashion at the moment. Be critical and try to think about it: do I need it, and do I really want it?

I AM AN HEIRLOOM

Where does the toy come from?

More than two thirds of toys are made in China. Again and again, experts are finding toxic substances in the plastic used. And in many factories workers have to work for 14 hours a day under terrible conditions. Yet another reason not to accumulate too much unnecessary stuff at home! By the way: try and go for fair trade toys, and toys that are ethically manufactured.

22.) Let the air out of balloons!

It's fun to launch balloons with your school or your club, but all those balloons will land as waste in nature, where they may accidentally get eaten by animals. Plastic tops and string are equally dangerous for animals, which may get caught in them. Perhaps you and your parents could suggest an alternative if somebody is planning to launch balloons? Sometimes, children get given balloons in the high street and they are used as party decorations. It's your choice: you may (sometimes) want to go without them.

23.) Plastic-free water fight!

Throwing water bombs in summer is fun. But sometimes, kids leave the remains of the burst balloons lying around instead of picking them up. Can you think of a better game? How about throwing wet sponges at each other?!

41

Single-use crockery

24.) No single-use crockery!

When they are having a barbecue in the park, at the school fete, or for birthday parties at home, many people use colourful single-use plates and cups. You should definitely avoid using plastic crockery anyway. But paper plates are also coated with plastic, and manufacturing them requires wood (for the fibres), and a lot of water and energy. Environmental organisations therefore state: all single-use crockery is waste! It is better to celebrate with crockery that can be washed up and reused.

25.) In a cone, please!

The tastiest packaging in the world is probably an ice cream cone. After all, you can munch it with your chocolate/ strawberry scoops. Then it's gone – unlike a plastic-coated tub with a plastic spoon.

YUMMY

ALSO YUMMY

AND DEFO ENVIRONMENTALLY FRIENDLY

26.) Snacks without waste!

Sometimes, you are out and about and hungry. Do you then buy food from a takeaway or a fast food restaurant? Then you can try to reduce (plastic) waste. Choose something that is in simple packaging. Carry your drink to the table without a plastic lid. Or you could buy a roll in a bakery and take it away without a bag... or bring a snack from home next time.

27.) No rubbish into nature!

Ice cream wrappers, crisp bags, and lolly sticks should always go into the bin, because plastic that someone carelessly throws away inland can be blown into a river by the wind. Then, it may eventually end up in the sea.

Waste

28.) Become a waste separation champion!

With a few simple tricks, you can help ensure that
the plastic from your recycling bin can be recycled
better.

ALUMINIUM

PLASTIC

YOGHURT

- In a lot of packaging, different types of plastic
are stuck together. So, before you throw
things away, separate the individual layers;
for example, the plastic film from the tray that
contained slices of cheese. This will make it easier for
the waste sorting plant to recognise both types of plastic.

- Remove the aluminium foil lid from the yoghurt pot and recycle
if possible. Remove advertising flyers from their plastic sleeves.
Tear clear plastic windows from paper bags and the adhesive
tape from cardboard boxes. Paper goes into the
paper bin, aluminium and plastics go into their
separate recycling bins.

PAPER

PLASTIC

- You are wasting energy if you wash out a
yoghurt pot before you put it in the recycling bin.
They should be "spoon-clean", just scraped out well.
This is sufficient!

CHEESE

← ALSO PLASTIC, BUT A DIFFERENT TYPE

PLASTIC

29.) Kitchen waste without plastics!

Sometimes, a mushy cucumber wanders into the food waste bin with its plastic wrapper, or small plastic stickers remain on apple skin. Even "biodegradable" plastic bags do not degrade sufficiently in composting plants. In the end, this is how a lot of microplastics end up in organic fertilisers and on our fields. What can you do? Make sure that no plastic of any kind gets into the food waste bin and collect organic waste in a small container without a bag. Of course, this container needs to be emptied every day. Perhaps you can do this for your family?

30.) Start a waste collection campaign!

One day in September each year is "International Coastal Cleanup Day", a day on which people all over the world clean up their coastlines. Many groups like the Marine Conservation Society are organising this in the UK. You can, of course, get active on any day, on your own, with friends or with school. Collecting litter is not just a good idea on beaches.

Real professionals

The Brown family manage to live nearly without any plastics. It is not even that difficult, say Mum Anneliese and twelve-year-old Noah.

When you take a look around your flat, Noah, can you still see things that are made of plastic?
Noah: Not many. Sometimes, I buy second-hand Lego – but there are no bits and pieces made from plastic that get broken quickly anyway. In our bathroom, we use a bar of soap instead of a bottle of shower gel. And in the kitchen we store our food in glass containers or in tins.

Why did you decide to ban plastic from your life?
Anneliese: A few years ago we were all ill over the Christmas holidays, one after the other. So, we spent two weeks inside the house... and collected a huge mountain of plastic waste during this time. I was really shocked and I started to find out more information about this issue: what are the actual effects of plastic on nature and on our health? Now I have made avoiding plastic my mission in life.

What are you now doing differently from other families?
Noah: We do not buy anything in plastic packaging. For example, we put vegetables in bio bags that my Mum made.

Anneliese: We hardly generate any waste because we only buy what we need. This means, for example, that we do not eat any fresh tomatoes in winter.

What do tomatoes have to do with plastic?
Anneliese: In winter, tomatoes grow in polytunnels with plastic film roofs in countries like Spain. These roofs are often blown into the sea. And, of course, these tomatoes are transported over long distances, for which they are packaged in plastic.

Do you feel that there are a lot of things you have to go without, Noah?
Noah: Not really. Tomatoes do taste better in the summer, after all. And we often find great solutions that work without plastic. Instead of buying chocolate bars, for example, we make our own Bounty bars. My mum doesn't deprive us of anything.

What do the other kids say if you have hardly any plastic toys or bring your lunch to school in a metal box?
Noah: Usually, nobody complains about it. But most children cannot imagine living without virtually any plastic themselves.

So why do you do it anyway?
Noah: I think it's important to help nature. After all, we are helping ourselves if we do that: if, one day, nature didn't exist any more, we humans wouldn't be able to live anymore either.

Let's get started!

You are now a plastics expert! You know how precious plastic is and that we should not waste it thoughtlessly. Everyone can make a contribution to ensure that less plastic is manufactured and less plastic gets into our environment. We only have this one wonderful Earth... and it urgently needs help! A lot of this needs to come from companies which manufacture items using plastics, but we can all do our bit! There are many organisations where you can find more information on the subject of plastic:

 The **WWF** is one of the largest organisations for the protection of nature in the world. They run many projects, including some to curb the flood of plastics in Southeast Asia. wwf.org.uk

GREENPEACE The **environmental organisation Greenpeace** regularly organises big campaigns against plastics. greenpeace.org.uk

 The organisation **Friends of the Earth** supports the fight against litter pollution of rivers and oceans. friendsoftheearth.uk

 And a new charity, **Kids against Plastic** is encouraging kids to take action against plastic pollution. kidsagainstplastic.co.uk